આશા

NOT YOUR MASI'S

GENERATION

HEALING THROUGH
SELF EXPLORATION,
AND REJECTING
GENERATIONAL
TRAUMA

WORKBOOK.
POEMS.
ESSAYS.
COMICS.
AND
THEORY.

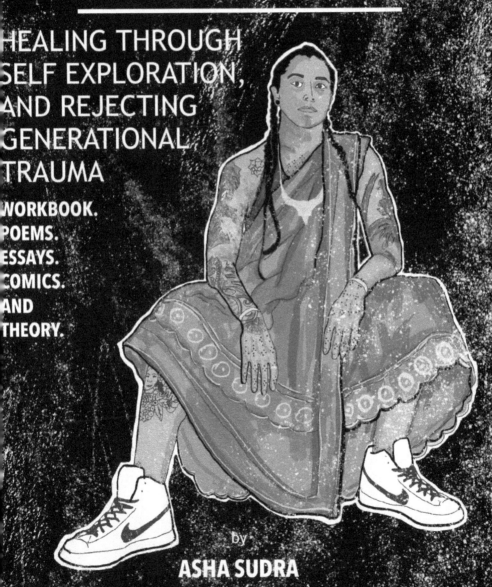

by
ASHA SUDRA

NOT YOUR MASI'S GENERATION

Healing through self exploration and rejecting generational trauma

by
ASHA SUDRA

NOT YOUR MASI'S GENERATION

Healing through self exploration and rejecting generational trauma

by
ASHA SUDRA

NOT YOUR MASI'S GENERATION

The Respect 360 Journal and The Respect Basics are trademarks and copyrighted material used with the permission of The Respect Institute(TM MARK) http://therespectinstitute.org

OUR MISSION IS TO MAKE RESPECT THE STATUS QUO.
WE GIVE YOUTH AND THEIR INFLUENCERS TOOLS TO
REDEFINE RESPECT AND BUILD SELF-RESPECT SO
THEY CAN BREAK CYCLES OF DISRESPECT AND THRIVE.

tell your TRUTH

know you're VALUABLE

have COURAGE

THE RESPECT BASICS

follow your PASSIONS

get HELP

trust your GUT

be COMPASSIONATE

set BOUNDARIES

THIS IS FOR YOU *

Womxn of color, introverts, intellectuals, BIPOC, qBIPOC, those struggling with mental health and options to cope, chronic illness survivors, artists, nerds, millennials, youth, those looking for both clinical and grounded approaches to addressing mental health.

Track list

Foreword..vi

Prelude..x

Intro..1

1: Frameworks of thought 7

2: BIPOC and mental health 11

Interlude: TELL YOUR TRUTH...........................19

3: Cognitive Distortions 29

    Filtering...33

    Polarizing/Absolute Thinking......................36

    Overgeneralization 39

    Mind Reading...42

    Catastrophizing...45

    Personalization..47

    Control Fallacies 49

    Fallacy of Fairness 52

    Blaming...54

    Should...58

    Emotional Reasoning....................................60

    Fallacy of Change 63

    Global Labeling...65

Being Right..67

Interlude: KNOW YOU'RE VALUABLE.........................69

4: Anger 79

5: Stress 91

    Different types of stress 93

    Coping Strategies 95

6: Forgiveness..101

Interlude: TRUST YOUR GUT 107

7: Evaluating Self 117

Interlude: FOLLOW YOUR PASSIONS........................125

8: Goal Setting 135

Interlude: HAVE COURAGE......................................149

9: Dialectical Behavioral Therapy............................159

10: Distress Tolerance 173

    Guidelines for Accepting Reality......................180

    Observing Your Breath Exercises 182

    Awareness Exercises 184

11: Emotional Regulation..187

    Emotion and Mindfulness Check-in 190

12: Interpersonal Effectiveness 199

    Priorities in Interpersonal Relationships...........207

    Stating Wants and Needs..................................208

    Keeping the Relationships 210

    Keeping Respect for Yourself 213

Assertive Bill of Rights...214

Variations of Communication............................215

Interlude: SET BOUNDARIES.................................223

13: Mindfulness..233

Purpose..241

Interlude: BE COMPASSIONATE.............................245

14: Duality..255

Interlude: BE OF SERVICE.......................................259

15: Final Reflection...263

Interlude: GET HELP...279

16: Notes/Glossary...289

Outro: Annotated Bibliography..............................303

Foreword

by
Reeta Loi

A book like this has long been needed and it could only be the powerful voice of someone with such rich intersections and experience as Asha Sudra that could create it.

The experiences of BIPOC and QBIPOC have been robbed and silenced for far too long and our experiences and histories erased. The trauma which we carry requires deep exploration and healing and this book acts as a guide.

As a queer South Asian gender-fluid womxn, I know only too well how this book would have changed my life for the better when I was younger. Having experienced multiple traumas as a child as well as being born a girl in a violently patriarchal culture and a person of colour in a white supremacist country are enough to cause compartmentalisation of self in anyone. However to then add queer into the mix, well let's just say the support systems were not there to support me or anyone like me anywhere in my education system, in my home or therapy practices at the time.

Mental health in the Global North is wildly myopic in its lack of inclusion of holistic practices that we are blessed with in the East. Medication is prescribed over meditation and the pharmaceutical giants continue to capitalise on not fixing us. The truth is, we must fix ourselves. This book brings together many threads of healing practices both Eastern and Western that I too have journeyed through in my adult life. It weaves in personal experience and poetry to open us up to Asha's own inner world, whilst providing exercises and tools to manage our mental health and illustrations and comics to help us relate in a variety of ways.

Working through this book I felt more understood than I have most of my life. Working through this book was made fun by the way it is intelligently structured, fusing art with exercises and personal storytelling. I gained a huge amount of self-knowledge through this book and crucially, I know I have a guide that I can come back to over and over again. Some of the guidance from Asha felt like the child in me was hearing from the grown up they wished they'd had in their life. Let's be clear, this brave book will transform and save lives of young people and adults the world over

As we heal, our mothers heal, our ancestors heal and the various strands of who we are connect and we become whole. This is our work and that this books exists, shows us what we are capable of when we dedicate our lives to our healing.

Every so often a truly great leader is presented to us. Asha Sudra is one we are blessed to have walk amongst us.

Prelude

First off, let me just say thank you for picking this book up. I wrote it for you, but more than anything, I put this together for me. Because I needed it. I've struggled with depression and anxiety for as long as I can remember. I would go through my cycles, attempt to ask for help, and ultimately decide I need to just deal with it on my own. It wasn't until about 9 years ago that I started to admit I needed help deciphering through the complex layers of my thoughts and started to go to therapy. Thank GAWD for her. I was wildly hesitant at first, but then I realized that going to therapy (if you have access) is hella grown. Shout out to the school counselor who dropped the science. Like, it's 2020, we all got this fucked up shit going on. Be grown and go unpack it somehow. It's not always easy to find someone that gives you what you need. I had to be really specific about finding a queer womxn of color and even followed her to a different facility when she moved to a city 45 minutes away, but the trust was there, and I'm really grateful for that, because she was often the only one I had/have to talk to.

For the last 16 years I have been dealing with a stomach disease called Gastroperesis, which delays stomach emptying causing a variety of painful symptoms. For the first 5 years I went undiagnosed as doctors simply treated my symptoms, due to the fact that the disease is rare and even more rare given my age and health at the time. The difficulty was that I also have Hemophilia C, which creates internal bleeding complications that were exacerbated by the throwing up from nausea and straining and stress of waking up at 3am every morning to throw up for years. To compound with everything, one time when throwing up, I severely injured several discs in my spine. Over the years there have been countless ER visits coupled with breakdowns and desires to give up. Dealing with the stresses of the world are already difficult, but complicated with invisible chronic illnesses and pain would send me into horrible spirals. Sometimes I wasn't sure if I would be able to get out of them.

When things would get real bad, and I finally had the courage to reach out to others beyond therapy, I didn't always get the response I was looking for from folx. They wouldn't always have the emotional capacity to have space to hear me fully, and if they did, they didn't always have the language to respond. I later realized I was expecting too much from an uninformed group, not because of a lack of intention, but simply because they didn't have the tools to navigate the difficult conversations that safety and mental health can bring. I would always do what all womxn of color do, which is be "resilient," as if it were a super power we are expected to have, and push through, carry on, keep rolling, or whatever other silly name or phrase we use when we don't address the hurt, the depression, or anxiety, and allow ourselves to heal. The reality is, as much as we wish we had that 'best friend' and supportive family, or amazing benefit package, it isn't promised. We also don't always have the tools to remind ourselves of things we already know or stop ourselves from spiraling.

When my therapist and I finally decided that things were getting much worse, not for lack of me trying or desire for change, I chose to enroll in an Intensive Outpatient Program to address my depression, suicidal thoughts, and anxiety. It was at the peak of depression after I had attempted for the first time to be honest with my family about my mental health issues and they laughed, rolled their eyes and shook their heads in my face. The amount of emotional drain that the event took on me stripped me of all super powers of resiliency. The thing was though, as much as I needed it, I found the program too clinical. I mean, it was literally in a clinic. The fluorescent lights made me sleepy, and gave me headaches; the chairs irritated the ruptured disc in my back. Everything was boring. Don't get me wrong, I love theory and pedagogy, the space just didn't vibe with me.

A lot of times, communities of color have looked down on higher education and pedagogy. The feelings are valid, as the expertise of many BIPOC communities have been disregarded, or stolen, and claimed. But by disregarding self-care and neglecting self-love, our communities have forgotten the ancestral traditions we once held. I had to breakdown and reach out to experts in the field to help me.

The program was functional, and I really hope it helped those in the group. While it offered valuable information, I didn't connect with the way they facilitated the classes. Not to mention it failed to see the intersection between mental health and chronic illness. They couldn't possibly consider all the factors of the 3, sometimes debilitating, conditions I suffer from. It felt too detached to soil. To my soil. Although I valued the information they would hand out, I didn't last through the full two-week recommendation. I didn't even make it to day 3. But I was still stuck, seeking, and now, desperate for something that focused on wellness and self-care. I knew for a fact however that I didn't want some appropriative and exploitive hippy retreat about peace, love and happiness with yoga workshops led by white people. I wanted something out there grounded in something indigenous, something ancestral which roots still stretched into the present. Something where Ayurvedic, Chinese, and Yoruban traditions could vibe with Hip-hop. For each chapter there is a hip hop lyric that came to mind when writing, and a Haiku reflecting my connection to the topic. I made this book because it's something I would want to use. Something that could address all of my intersections as I learned more about my depression and mental health struggles.

This is for womxn of color, for introverts, intellectuals, poets of color, queer people of color, academics, those struggling with mental health and options to cope, youth, artists, nerds, millennials, those looking for both clinical and grounded approaches to addressing mental health. Everything is rooted in theory, and nothing is promised to fix it all. Let the book be a guide. A facilitation. A reminder. It's what I will use when I see the spiral form. I hope it helps.

Intro:

"You need to git up, git out and git something"
(Outkast)

"You need git up, git out and git something
How will you make it if you never even try
You need to git up, git out and git something
'Cause you and I got to do for you and I"
- Southernplayalisticadillacmuzik
1994

1

Hip-hop taught unique
pillars of Outkasts freely;
run to their own beat.

When I realized that the intensive outpatient program (IOP) through my insurance wasn't going to work, and I struggled to find a program that fit my needs, I decided to turn to books, because the intellectual, nerd, and academic in me yearned to understand something that seemed so out of my control at times. I found poems, and essays, and Hip-hop, prose, and comics all about self-love and mental health. Everything I found had its levels of relatability, but it was missing some key components that the pedagogy of the IOP provided. One part of my safety plan is to stay engaged with projects and creative expressions, and so I dove into creating a book that encompassed all of the components of the various books I was reading in addition to the theory that was presented in the group therapy sessions.

Throughout the book there are opportunities for you to engage in exercises, evaluate yourself, set goals, reflect on progress and define certain aspects of your wants and needs that will hopefully directly impact your mental health. The book begins with the stigma of mental health in communities of color. It was important to address that first. There is no room for any of that antiquated thinking here. Then the book dives directly into theory and suggestions for management, but it's packaged as an appetizing little snack, in the form of comics, poems and anecdotes. Because the world expects so much from womxn of color, often times a lot of our depression manifests in cognitive distortions. For this reason, the book explores Cognitive Behavioral Therapy, which was coined by Aaron T. Beck in the 1960s, and since changed, tweaked and modified by others throughout psychological discovery.

Reading through the various layers of thought distortions really helped ground some of the shame and embarrassment I was having around my depression. Because it's more than just the mind, the world around us causes so much stress, anger and hurt which also directly impacts our health. Through it all, we have to learn to forgive ourselves. After breaking down some of the cognitive behavioral therapy, the book provides an opportunity for you to evaluate yourself and where you're at. After establishing some understanding of self, the next step is to set some goals, both short term and long term.

Once the goals are set, the book explores Dialectical Behavior Therapy (DBT), made famous by psychologist Marsha M. Linehan in the late 1980s. These chapters provide a breakdown of the 4 different components of DBT (distress tolerance, emotional regulation, interpersonal effectiveness, and mindfulness). Again, while everything is rooted in theory, I try to provide you with the information in an accessible way.

After the break down of theory and hopefully time for folx to work on their goals, with the understanding that not everything will work for everyone, people will have a chance to reflect on their progress. I first came across the Respect Institute handbook in a workshop led by De-Bug supporting families of those affected by police killings in San Jose. The founder of Respect Institute, Courtney Macavinta, believes in equitable mental health that is accessible for all. Each component of the Respect Institute handbook seeks to provide youth and adults with opportunities to reflect and understand oneself better. After that workshop back in 2017, I sought her out to get copies for my students and she hooked me up with multiple copies, including Spanish copies for parents. She has continued to support me and I'm grateful to have her work included in this book.

Finding strategies to help manage depression is like putting together puzzle pieces from an image that changes constantly. One thing that worked before, might not work again. Sometimes doing something that is different is the best thing you can do. Hopefully this book presents a menu of things that you can try and evaluate yourself to see what helps the most.

Enjoy the journey. Be open to it. I was wildly hesitant at first, so I get it. Allow the art and creative and reflective thought processes of the book take precedence above everything.

Chapter 1:

Frameworks of Thought

"I say hypothetical because it's only theory"
(Boogie Down Productions)

"I say hypothetical because it's only theory
My theory, so take a minute now to hear me"
-Criminal Minded
1987

Underground Hip-hop.
Intention; quests for knowledge;
the seeds planted home.

I consider myself a student for life. I love pedagogy, theory, and all things academic. In trying to understand my own struggles with mental health, I had to honor all parts of me, including the one who wanted to understand my feelings from a sociological perspective. When I entered into the outpatient program, they handed me a folder full of names and studies of theory I was unfamiliar with. Cognitive behavioral therapy and Dialectical Behavior therapy are two frameworks that this book breaks down. My attempt is to create a platform that provides the information in accessible and tangible ways, such as poems and comics.

As my experience of being a teacher has taught me, the best way to learn is to tap into the multiple modalities of the individual. Because I created this book with myself in mind, I knew I needed more than just theory, but to provide a space for processing and accountability as well. The Respect Institute has created an educational resource that enables its participant to be active in social emotional learning about the self and how one interacts with others. By combining the processing of theory, added with contextual application, and written accountability, I truly feel that we can take on understanding our own struggles with mental health.

The final framework of understanding comes from accessing our own ancestral practices as a form of decolonization. Being mindful of indigenous medicines and traditions allow us to truly embark on healing the generational trauma we experience daily. Recognize that the stigma of eastern medicine comes from a white supremacist ideology that during the first wave of racist "orientalism" invalidated it as legitimate, to now, during the second wave, which is full of co-optation and appropriation. RESIST. Find authentic practitioners and explore practices that would crumble the medical industrial complex. I recommend through me telling my story to you that you seek out your own path that honors your ancestry and the healing practices that they once used.

10

Chapter 2:

BIPOC and mental health

"I've been dealing with depression ever since an
adolescent"
(Kendrick Lamar)

"*Everybody lack confidence, everybody lack*

confidence

How many times our potential was anonymous?

How many times the city making me promises?

So I promise this

And I love myself"

-To Pimp a Butterfly

2015

Cant keep denying†
the community struggles†
for a minute too*

The one and only time I ever tried to explain that I was struggling with my mental health to my family, it just didn't work. After some heated arguments, and me realizing my message wasn't coming across, I looked at my mom with defeat.

ITS IN YOUR HEAD

LA started to become less and less of a home
over time.*
Less and less a source of comfort
and instead a breeding site for anxiety.*
Litters of shady pups trying to outlast a Los
Angeles sun.*
Survival of the fittest
into submission.*

I am not myself here.*

I crab crawled away
into whatever bucket or arm that felt
validating.*
Affirmations found in afflictions.*
Vice versus virtue
vicious thoughts seemed to
search and pry at every glimpse of doubt.*

The foundation of who I am
strangered into exile.*
Found through intention and honesty.*
Finally seeking refuge in
gas lit corridors of chance
once taken
to alleviate invisible pressures of darkness.*

I tried to explain why I don't call it home.
Why I rarely come back to this place at all
and why I don't stay long.
The coyotes of the San Fernando Valley
laughed.
Ganged up.
Some because they had never heard language
like mine.
Talk of the mind had never been given
space.
Ancestors before had always followed the
same paths
and carried on
because survival.

Some told me it was in my head.
That my feelings I finally named after 30
years
didn't exist.
Eye rolls snowballed into avalanched
confidence.
I was smothered.
Gasping for breath
fighting my way out of flesh of blood
diseased.

Infectious.

Hollywood is a global phenomenon.
The facade of a mind sound.
Award winning acting.
Writing narratives that ignore humanity in
bodies of color.
Removing a pouring of emotion symptomatic
of history's disregard for melanin.

I had to take space to decolonize.
We have to make space to decolonize.

I can't hear the ancestors here.

I try so hard to listen but they are drowned
out in unhealthy tradition.
Instead I'm filled with these cognitive
distortions
and they are screaming.

I miss them.
I know they have answers and healing and
medicine and stories to be remembered
I've been taught to ignore.
I long for a chance to be near tongues close
to my blood; to listen so tastes can
recognize the past.

Distance from LA reminds me I am not who
they told me I am not.

Distance from LA reminds me I am whole.
Despite attempts to convince me my
depression makes me otherwise.

Interlude

TELL YOUR TRUTH

tell your TRUTH

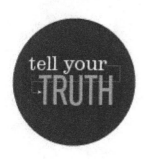

What is a difficult experience you have come through stronger?
What happened?

What are ways you're different from your friends and family?

If you were to write a book, what would it be about?

Feelings	Needs	
Afraid	Acceptance	Shelter
Confused	Appreciation	Peace
Embarrassed	Affection	Humor
Tense	Love	Inspiration
Annoyed	Respect	Independence
Angry	Compassion	Hope
Sad	Safety	Learning
Vulnerable	Trust	To Matter
Scared	Food	Understanding
In Pain	Sleep	Friendship
Yearning		
Tired	*More examples at the Center for*	
Nervous	*Nonviolent Communication at cnvc.org.*	

My Feelings, Needs and Values

Take a moment to review the list of feelings and needs

What are you feeling right now?

What do you need right now?

My values—the rules I live by—are ...

To live by my values each day, I need to ...

I express my thoughts best by (e.g., writing, singing, painting) ...

I express my feelings best by ...

I feel totally free when I am ...

Final Thoughts

I'm strong at **Tell Your Truth** because I ...

I can practice **Tell Your Truth** more by ...

Chapter 3

Cognitive Distortions

"My mind is playing tricks on me"
(Geto Boys)

"Day by day it's more impossible to cope"
-We can't be stopped
1991

Hot summers rolling
black out consciousness flowing.
90s mind plays tricks.

Almost everyone has given in to a type of cognitive distortion at one time or another. To me, it's when my mind sees and experiences the world through my insecurities. I miss things, and I build that perspective into a narrative that I use to define myself, regardless of what may actually be occurring. Sometimes it's a combination of both, where something unfair is happening, and that feeds into my insecurities. I have to check myself and re-evaluate what's going on, Sometimes a situation that is unfair will occur, but after resolution, cognitive distortions prevent me from getting out of the spiral, and it can lead to extended periods of depression. I really struggle with feelings of isolation, which are exacerbated by the way cognitive distortions manifest in my mind. As you look at the list, you may well recognize one or more from your own experience, and something you may recognize in others. There are situations in which patterns of such distortions lead us to experience the world in ways that can worsen feelings of anxiety, anger or depression. These patterns are usually very well hidden from ourselves. When we can catch ourselves in our own patterns of distorted thinking, we give ourselves the opportunity to replace the old thinking with a more rational alternative. We can start to move away from distortions, and closer to a more realistic way of experiencing the world.

COGNITIVE DISTORTIONS:

FILTERING

You take negative details and magnify them while filtering out all positive aspects of a situation.

NO NEED TO MAGNIFY/SHIFT FOCUS

Stuck in a mental groove,

     Focusing on things from your environment that typically tend to

         frighten,

              sadden,

                   or anger you

To conquer filtering you will have to deliberately shift focus.

You can shift focus in two ways:

First, place your attention on coping strategies to deal with the problem rather than obsessing about the problem itself.

Second, categorize your primary mental theme as: loss, injustice, or _____(fill in your own theme).
If your theme is danger, focus on things in your environment that represent comfort and safety.

When you are filtering you usually end up magnifying your problems.

To combat magnifying, stop using words like terrible, awful, disgusting, horrendous, etc.

Stop saying "I can't stand it" and start saying "I can cope" and "no need to magnify"

POLARIZING/ABSOLUTE THINKING

Things are black and white, good or bad. Perfect or failure, there is no middle ground

NO BLACK AND WHITE JUDGMENTS/THINK IN PERCENTAGES

People are not either happy or sad, loving or rejecting, brave or cowardly, smart or stupid.

They

fall somewhere

along a continuum.

They are a little bit of each.

Human beings are just too complex to be reduced to dichotomous judgments.

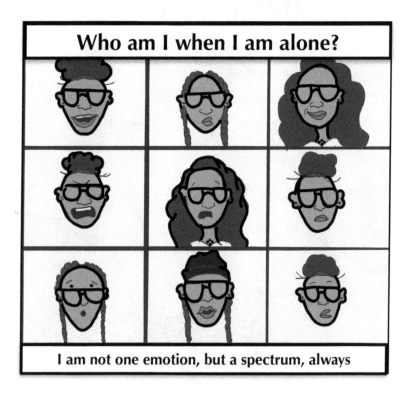

We have to stop living in binaries.

If you have to make these judgments think in terms of percentages. 30% of me is struggling with suicidal thoughts, but 70% of me is holding on and coping..."

COGNITIVE DISTORTIONS

OVERGENERALIZATION

You come to a general conclusion based on a single incident or piece of evidence. If it happens once, you expect it to happen over and over again.

QUANTIFY/EVIDENCE FOR CONCLUSIONS/THERE ARE NO ABSOLUTES

This is the tendency to exaggerate. You can fight this tendency by quantifying instead of using words like huge, awful, massive, minuscule, etc.

You can examine how much evidence you really have for your conclusion. If the conclusion is based on one or two cases, a single mistake, or one small symptom, then throw it out till you have more convincing proof.

If you overgeneralize, you think in absolutes.

Avoid statements and assumptions that use words like "every, all, always, none, never, everybody, and nobody.

Be particularly sensitive to absolute predictions about the future (no one will ever love me). They are extremely dangerous because they can become self-fulfilling prophecies.

MIND READING

Without them saying, you assume how people are feeling and why they act the way they do, and you know how people are feeling toward you

CHECK IT OUT/EVIDENCE FOR CONCLUSION

This is the tendency to make inferences about how people feel and think.

In the long run, you are probably better off making no inferences about people at all.

Either believe what they tell you or hold no belief at all until some conclusive evidence comes your way.

Treat all your notions about people as hypotheses to be tested and checked out by asking them.

CATASTROPHIZING

You expect disaster. You notice or hear about a problem and start "what if's" (tragedy, something happens to you)

REALISTIC ODDS

This is the royal road to anxiety.

As soon as you catch yourself, make an honest assessment of the situation in terms of odds or percent of probability.

Looking at odds helps you realistically evaluate whatever is frightening you.

PERSONALIZATION

Thinking that everything people do or say is some kind of
reaction to you. You also compare yourself to others, trying to
determine who's smarter, better looking etc.

CHECK IT OUT/EVIDENCE FOR CONCLUSION/WHY RISK COMPARISONS

Force yourself to prove what other people's actions have to do with you.

If you can't ask the person, make no conclusions unless you are satisfied that you have reasonable evidence and proof.

It is also important to abandon the habit of comparing yourself-negatively or positively-with other people.

Comparisons are unhealthy.

Your worth doesn't depend on being better than others.

CONTROL FALLACIES

If you feel externally controlled, you see yourself as helpless, a victim of fate. The fallacy of internal control has you responsible for the pain and happiness of everyone around you

I MAKE IT HAPPEN/EACH ONE IS RESPONSIBLE

You are only responsible for what happens in your world.

The omnipotence fallacy is the opposite side of the coin from external control fallacy.

Instead of everyone else being responsible for your problems, you are responsible for everyone else's problems.

The key to overcoming the omnipotence fallacy is to recognize that each one is responsible for themselves.

Also remember, part of respecting others includes letting them lives their own lives, suffer their own pains, and solve their own problems.

COGNITIVE DISTORTIONS

FALLACY OF FAIRNESS

You feel resentful because you think you know what's fair, but other people wont agree with you

PREFERENCE VS. FAIRNESS

The word fair is a nice disguise for personal preferences and wants.

Be honest with yourself and the other person.

Say what you want or prefer without dressing it up in the fallacy of fairness.

> **I gave it some time. I stepped back and continued to show love. They accepted me. With all of my flaws**

BLAMING

You hold other people responsible for your pain, or take the
other track and blame yourself for every problem

I MAKE IT HAPPEN/EACH ONE IS RESPONSIBLE

It is your responsibility to state your needs, say no, or go elsewhere.

The other person is not responsible for knowing or helping you meet you needs.

Focus on the choices you have made. Examine what options you have for coping with it.

There is a difference between taking responsibility and turning the blame on yourself.

Taking responsibility means accepting the consequences of your own choices.

Blaming yourself means attacking your own
self-esteem and labeling yourself bad if you make a mistake.

Taking responsibility doesn't
imply that you are also responsible for what happens to others.

Blaming yourself for another person's problems is a
form of self-aggrandizement. It means you think you are having
more impact on their lives than they are.

Sometimes you have to clip the strings yourself

SHOULDS

You have a list of ironclad rules about how you and other people should act. People who break the rules anger you and you feel guilty if you violate the rules

FLEXIBLE RULES/FLEXIBLE VALUES

Re-examine and question any personal rules or expectations that include the words should, ought, or must.

Flexible rules and expectations don't use these words because there are always exceptions and special circumstances.

You may get irritated when people don't act according to your values, but your personal values belong to only you.

People just aren't all the same.

Focus on each person's uniqueness, their particular needs, limitations, fears, and pleasures.

COGNITIVE DISTORTIONS

EMOTIONAL REASONING

You believe that what you feel must be true- automatically. (If you feel stupid you must be stupid)

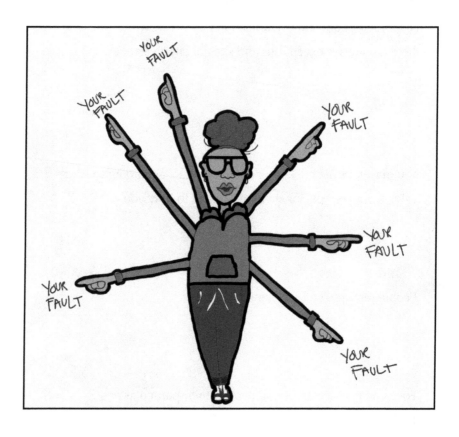

FEELINGS CAN LIE

What you feel is entirely dependent on what you think.

IF you have distorted thoughts, your feelings wont have validity.

Your feelings can lie to you.

If you're feeling depressed or anxious all the time, it's almost certain they are lying to you.

There is nothing automatically true about what you feel.

Be skeptical about your feelings and examine them for distorted thoughts.

FALLACY OF CHANGE

You expect that other people will change to suit you if you just pressure them enough. You need to change people because your happiness depends entirely on them.

I MAKE IT HAPPEN

Your happiness depends on you, on each of the decisions you make.

You cannot expect other people to change to accommodate that.

You have to decide whether to leave or to stay, say yes or no.

Each person makes it happen for themselves.

COGNITIVE DISTORTIONS

GLOBAL LABELING

Generalize one or two qualities in a negative global judgment

When the left side of the brain has all the power, no one wins

BE SPECIFIC

Rather than applying global labels, you can limit your
observations to a specific case.

Ask yourself if a case is always true, or only true now, or only
true some of the time.

COGNITIVE DISTORTIONS

BEING RIGHT

You are continually on trial to prove that your opinions and
actions are correct. Being wrong is unthinkable

ACTIVE LISTENING

If you've always got to be right, you don't listen.

The key to overcoming being right is active listening.

As an active listener you participate in communication by repeating what you think you've heard in order to make sure you really understand what's been said to you.

A proportionately great amount of time is spent trying to understand the other person than devising your own rebuttals and attacks.

Remember that other people believe what they are saying as strongly as you believe in your convictions, and there is not always one right answer.

Interlude

KNOW YOU'RE VALUABLE

know you're VALUABLE

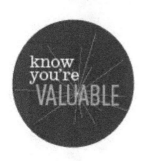

What do your choices about how you spend your time say about how you value yourself?

What do you value about yourself that it feels like others haven't appreciated in the past?

What do you consider your greatest accomplishments so far?

My Value

One reason I matter to others is ...

One way I matter to the whole world is ...

One way I can treat myself like I matter is ...

One way I can treat others like they matter is ...

Disrespect vs. Respect

List disrespect and respect examples.

- Under Disrespect: List the top ways you and/or others have treated you like you're not valuable. Then list all the ways you're being hard on yourself today.

- Under Respect: Write one way you can value yourself next to each disrespect example on the left.

Disrespect	Respect

One place I feel safe is ...

One person I know loves and accepts me is ...

Final Thoughts

I'm strong at **Know You're Valuable** because I ...

I can practice **Know You're Valuable** more by ...

Chapter 4:

Anger

Don't push me, cause I'm close to the edge
(Grandmaster Flash & the Furious Five)

"I'm trying not to lose my head

It's like a jungle sometimes

It makes me wonder how I keep from goin' under"

-The Message

1982

Check your own thinking:
the world is full of anger.
Conditions harmful.

HANDLING ANGER

LISTEN TO YOUR
WARNING SIGNALS

BODY SIGNALS

Clamming up, blushing, shallow breathing,
shaking, muscular tension, headache,
laughing for no reason, a rise in voice pitch,
etc. Look for your own

I get super sweaty

FEELING SIGNALS

Anger is usually the second emotion we have. The first may be hurt, disappointment, and frustration. What feelings usually precede your anger?

I often feel hurt and disappointed

Unrealistic expectations can do that

MIND SIGNALS

These are usually triggered by let down expectations of others or, we also may evaluate and judge another or ourselves. What are your mind signals?

BECOME AWARE OF HOW YOU USUALLY REACT

PHYSICALLY ACTING OUT

Scream, kick, hit or abuse/verbally blame or insult

When I used to get angry, I would get so frustrated that I would hit myself. It was terrible.

INTERNALIZE

Over/under eat, get sick, withdraw, get depressed, neglect
yourself or others, sleep, don't sleep, abuse drugs/alcohol.

DECIDED ON A PLAN, WHAT CAN YOU DO INSTEAD?

TAKE RESPONSIBILITY

Own your feelings

STATE YOUR FEELINGS AND NEEDS

Use I statements

This can sometimes sound corny, I get it.

But the reality is no one can deny your experience of feeling a certain emotion.

So for example, when I feel dismissed when I don't get to participate in planning an event, instead of yelling at them for not including me, potentially causing   them to put up a guard, I can let them know,

"I feel really hurt when I'm not included in planning. I'd like to be a part of the process so I am aware"

So the equation is that you state your feelings first and connect it to an action, then, if you have the capacity, offer what you would prefer. It can sound different in different situations, but stay true to yourself.

TAKE A TIME OUT
Calm yourself down before trying to resolve the situation. It's ok to take a breath and evaluate where your head is at.

DIRECT ACTION

Do something positive to release your energy

If I stay in the same place, I'll drown.

I have to physically move.

Sometimes its a walk with my dog, Coltrane,

Sometimes its going to buy some boba

PREVENTION

Regularly practice stress reduction techniques to keep your stress levels down

This is where we have to tap into our ancestors.

I regularly see a Chinese medicine doctor, which includes making an herbal tea and acupuncture

Therapy is the second most consistent thing in my life next to having a dog, both save me.

Every time.

AFFIRMATION

Praise your effect and successes

This one is the hardest for me, because self-
affirmation was not something I learned as a
child growing up in a South Asian home, but
I feel better when I surround myself with
people who love me, because I love my
friends
I love my growth
I love my art

Anger is tricky. Admittedly I'm a very angry person by nature. To be honest, inside, it feels like I carry more anger than just my own. I feel like I carry the anger of my mother, and the abuse she endured. That I carry the anger of family exile, struggle and trauma.

Defining anger is not easy. The way it is both imposed and self-imposed however is something I think is important to be conscious of. How we see ourselves in our anger allows for us to respond to it.

Some of the anger I have experienced has propelled me into better versions of myself. It, in my eyes, has benefited me and my commitment to justice. However, I know for a fact my anger has acted against me, against my relationships and perhaps most importantly, against my health. I carry a heavy resentment for being so sick. I've had more anger filled breakdowns in ER rooms before I was 30 than anyone should ever have to. I spent my 21st birthday in the hospital throwing up blood from internal bleeding, alone. I hold an anger that I wake up every day in pain. I can't escape that anger, but I see how it brings me down and feeds into my insecurities.

I can't fix it. But I am aware of it. And I am trying to work on how to respond to it. It's hard though. Really hard.

Chapter 5:

Stress

I really know how it feels to be stressed out
(A Tribe Called Quest)

"I really know how it feels to be, stressed out,

stressed out

When you're face to face with your adversity

I really know how it feels to be, stressed out, stressed

out

We're gonna make this thing work out eventually"

-Beats, Rhymes, and Life

1996

Hip-hop has power.
Validate resilience.
Music sees people.

DIFFERENT TYPES OF STRESSORS

Environmental changes: weather, noise, traffic, and pollution, white supremacy

Social: work, school or program deadlines, financial problems, interviews, relationship issues, loss of loved ones, white supremacy

Physiological: aging process, menopause in women, illness, accidents, lack of exercise, poor nutrition, sleep disturbance, white supremacy

Cognitive: distortions, white supremacy

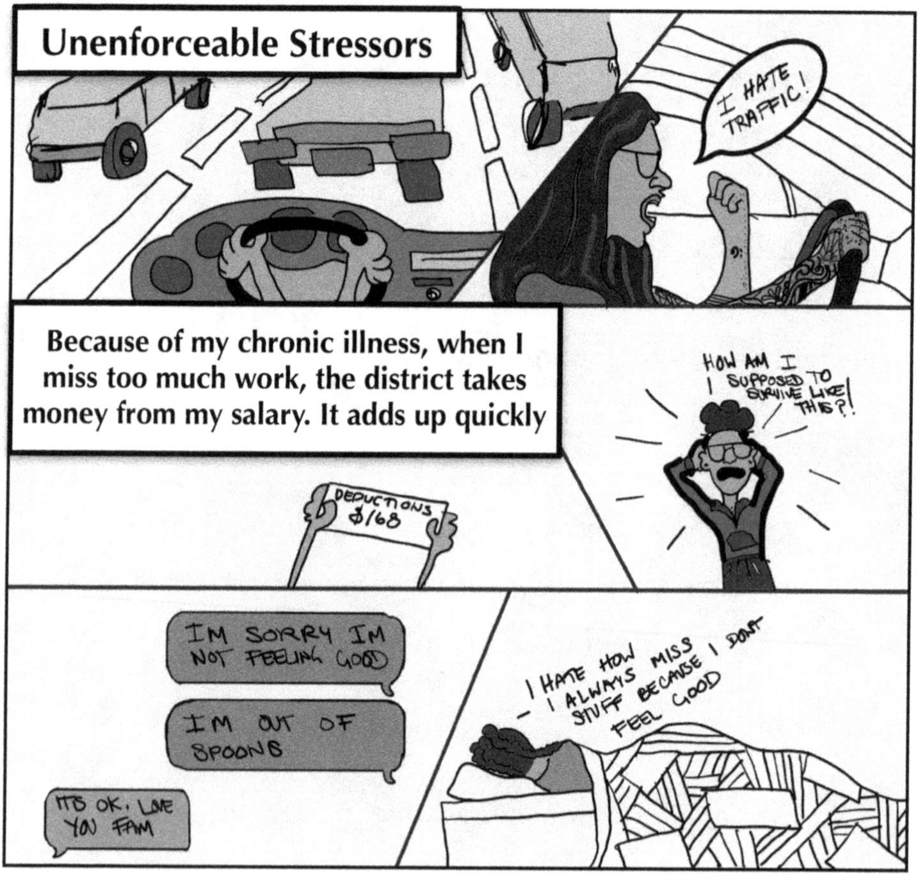

Unenforceable Stressors
I HATE TRAFFIC!
Because of my chronic illness, when I miss too much work, the district takes money from my salary. It adds up quickly
DEDUCTIONS $168
HOW AM I SUPPOSED TO SURVIVE LIKE THIS?!
IM SORRY IM NOT FEELING GOOD
IM OUT OF SPOONS
ITS OK. LOVE YOU FAM
I HATE HOW I ALWAYS MISS STUFF BECAUSE I DONT FEEL GOOD

COPING STRATEGIES:

MIND CLEARING EXERCISES

Lie on the floor with your feet up on a chair. Place a cool washcloth on your face or over your eyes. Focus on a peaceful word, thought, saying or image. Stay there for 5 minutes.

Read inspirational thoughts, quotes or poems. Collect them and keep them in a notebook that you can refer to.

Tell you mind to STOP. Focus on something that is happening in the present so you are not caught up on what happened in the past...

Change your choice of words from I should to I prefer, or I am choosing to. Be aware of the differences between your wants and needs.

Think of 3 things you are grateful for.

ROUTINES AND ATTITUDES TO KEEP STRESS LEVELS DOWN

Plan pleasant times you can count on with others

Practice daily positive affirmations. Practice or share these affirmations with others

Recognize your successes

Evaluate your expectations of yourself. Be mindful of
unrealistic ones.

Be honest with yourself.

Share feelings and experiences with family or friends,
but be aware they may not have the capacity,
communication skills, or response you are looking
for.

Resolve conflicts or difficulties as they arise instead of putting them off or denying that there's a problem. Resolve conflicts in a respectful manner, where you maintain your dignity, but recognize when you are being disrespected.

Be assertive. It is a skill that can be learned.

Chapter 6:

Forgiveness

It may sound crazy*, but I forgive you
(Diana Ross)

"Every day is a new day"

-*Every day is a new day*

1999

---

*I think it's really important to begin to see and call out the casual use
of the word "crazy". It is harmful, limiting and down right
appropriative. Generationally, as we learn more about the human mind
and it's capabilities, we also have to adjust our use of language. This is
one that is long over due and needs to go. Respect to the Queen Diana
Ross.

Diana describes
love with a timbre of voice.
own your self respect.

FORGIVENESS

Forgiveness does not condone or enable

Know exactly how you feel about what happened and be able to articulate what is not OK about that situation. Tell people who are trusted and have capacity. You may need time to process how you are feeling. Don't force yourself into dialogue with someone until you are ready. Do not submit power to someone who has caused you harm without being secure in your position.

Commit to yourself to do what you have to do to feel better. Forgiveness is for you, and not anyone else.

Forgiveness does not necessarily mean reconciliation

Give up on expecting things from other people, or your life. Recognize the 'unenforceable rules" you have for your health or how you or other people must behave.

Put your energy into looking for another way to get your positive goals met than through the experience that has hurt you. Don't just mentally replay your hurt.

Unenforceable rules: things that you expect, but cannot control (how people act, the weather , etc.)

Interlude

TRUST YOUR GUT

trust your GUT

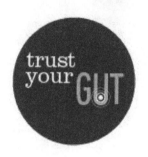

What happens in your gut when you feel scared?

What happens in your gut when you feel nervous?

What makes trusting your gut sometimes difficult?

What is an example in your life of making the same choice over and over again even though you keep getting hurt?

What happens when you trust your gut?

My Gut

For 5 minutes, free write or draw everything on your mind and what you're feeling in your "gut" right now   What feelings, needs or worries do you "hear"?

My gut sends me messages by ... It can feel like ...

I don't listen to my gut when ...

When I don't listen to my gut, what happens is ...

It is important that I trust my gut because ...

In five years I think I will be ...

People I trust to support me in achieving my goals are ...

Final Thoughts

I'm strong at **Trust Your Gut** because I ...

I can practice **Trust Your Gut** more by ...

Chapter 7:

Evaluating self

"I know that I'm always gonna hold me down"
(Lizzo)

"Cause I'm my own soulmate
I know how to love me
I know that I'm always gonna hold me down
Yeah, I'm my own soulmate
No, I'm never lonely
I know I'm a queen but I don't need no crown
Look up in the mirror like damn she the one"
-Cuz I Love you
2019

Who ever doubted
their sense of self completely;
you are never still

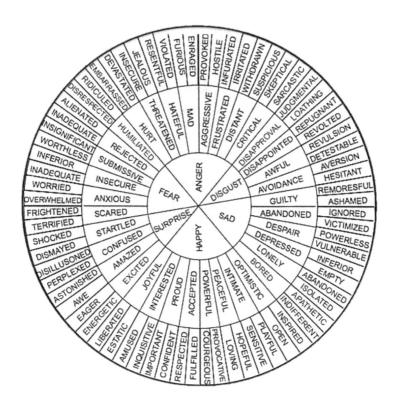

Plutchik's "Wheel of Emotions"

Manifestation List

Use this chart to evaluate how you manage. Mark each
behavior along a spectrum as it corresponds to you

Behavior

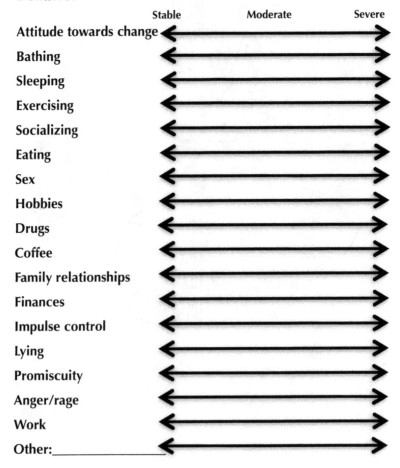

	Stable	Moderate	Severe
Attitude towards change	←		→
Bathing	←		→
Sleeping	←		→
Exercising	←		→
Socializing	←		→
Eating	←		→
Sex	←		→
Hobbies	←		→
Drugs	←		→
Coffee	←		→
Family relationships	←		→
Finances	←		→
Impulse control	←		→
Lying	←		→
Promiscuity	←		→
Anger/rage	←		→
Work	←		→
Other:_____	←		→

Daily Mood Log

Purpose: To help you process painful emotions such as loneliness, depression, anger, guilt, frustration, worry and fear. There are 4 basic steps. Use the emotion wheel to identify feelings.

1. Describe the upsetting event. Write a brief description of the situation or problem. It can be simple stuff like coming home to an empty place or an argument with someone you care about.
    a. Make sure you are specific as to person, place and time.

2. Identify your negative feelings. Record your negative emotions and rate how intense they are between 0-100%. For example, you might be hurt 80%; angry 75%; disappointed 90%; , etc.

3. Change your thoughts. Write down the thoughts associated with your feelings. Number them consecutively and indicate how much you believe each thought between 0-100%
    a. In the middle column identify the distortions in your thought, using the distortions listed in chapter 3.
    b. Substitute other thoughts that are more positive or realistic. Indicate how much you believe each of them between 0-100%. Finally, evaluate how much you believe you Negative thoughts 0-100%

4. Outcome: Indicate how much better you feel now. Cross out your original estimates and put new ones.

Daily Mood Log

Situation:		Cognitive distortions:	
Beginning emotion/s:	**Initial Negative Thoughts:**	**Balanced Thoughts:**	**Ending emotion/s:**
Situation:		Cognitive distortions:	
Beginning emotion/s:	**Initial Negative Thoughts:**	**Balanced Thoughts:**	**Ending emotion/s:**
Situation:		Cognitive distortions:	
Beginning emotion/s:	**Initial Negative Thoughts:**	**Balanced Thoughts:**	**Ending emotion/s:**

Daily Mood Log

Situation:		Cognitive distortions:	
Beginning emotion/s:	Initial Negative Thoughts:	Balanced Thoughts:	Ending emotion/s:
Situation:		Cognitive distortions:	
Beginning emotion/s:	Initial Negative Thoughts:	Balanced Thoughts:	Ending emotion/s:
Situation:		Cognitive distortions:	
Beginning emotion/s:	Initial Negative Thoughts:	Balanced Thoughts:	Ending emotion/s:

Interlude

FOLLOW YOUR PASSIONS

follow your
PASSIONS

What inspires you most in the world?

What goals do you have for your life/family/education?

What is your favorite way to spend free time?

What are ways you can build a better support network for your passions?

My Passions

I feel best when I'm …

I often lose track of time when I'm …

Someday I want to learn to ...

because I want ...

Something I'm good at but want to practice more is ...

because ...

My Inspiration

Passions are usually things that move or inspire us in some way. One way to capture those feelings is to write a poem or song or draw a picture about something you're passionate about or that moves you. Start here:

My Future Self

Write a letter to yourself from your **Future Self**, who is 10 years older than you are now. What encouraging words, suggested boundaries, and advice does he/she have for you?

Final Thoughts

I'm strong at **Follow Your Passions** because I ...

I can practice **Follow Your Passions** more by ...

Chapter 8:

Goal setting

All night till the morning we dream so long
(Lupe Fiasco)

"So no matter what you been through

No matter what you into

No matter what you see

when you look outside your window

Brown grass or green grass

Picket fence or barbed wire

Never ever put them down

You just lift your arms higher

Raise 'em 'til your arms tired

Let em' know you're there

That you struggling and survivin'

That you gonna persevere yeah"

-Lasers

2010

It just felt freeing,
and now, years later, I still
want to feel that way.

Goal Setting and Self-Monitoring

Goal:

	Steps	Obstacles	Plan	Timeframe
1.				
2.				
3.				
4.				
5.				

	Strengths	Resources
1.		
2.		
3.		

Goal Setting and Self-Monitoring Progress Update
(2-6 weeks depending on plan)

Goal Changes (if any):

	Progress and Accomplishments	Planned Adjustments
1.		
2.		
3.		
4.		
5.		
	Maintenance Plan:	Timeframe:
1.		
2.		
3.		

IMAGINE RADICALLY

I asked her
in broken Gujarati and English
needing my mother to fill voids of words we both
didn't understand
Ba,
"If you could have done anything with your life
money, family, tradition aside…
what would you have wanted to do?"

Questions
lost in translation
not for lack of words
but for lack of dreams.
Confusion
context unknown and
inconceivable.

The perplexed look on her face
sent me into internal tears.
Tearing at my soul
knowing she was never fully given hers.
Identity that would never belong to her because
she was always owned.

Belonged to families she had never met.

Ba came from extreme poverty in Kenya.
With the loss of her mother at the age of 2
the remarriage of her father
and subsequent step siblings to follow
she was a pawn.
A trading card.
Not a rare hologram
demanding recognition of value and fairness
no.
At 15
a dowry
that would never be enough
drowning in suffocation
she never had a voice.
Told
this family has more than we do.
It will be a better life for you than it would be here.
Besides
there are so many other kids we have to care for.

Given to
in-laws that would doubt her contribution

claiming
tainting
and devaluing of caste pride.
Constantly looked down upon.
Constantly striving for acceptance.
Forced to learn the ways of a family
who had more than she ever did
as to denounce her own poverty stricken shame.

So when I asked her
"What are your life dreams?"
she had no answer.
No
conception
of a dream without responsibility
without expectation
without reigns
rain would come and fall
but she never learned what control felt like.
So when I asked her
"What are your life dreams?"
Immediately she wished for her family to be taken
care of.
To not have to worry if her children could afford
rent that month.

I tried to construct the fantasy
in which all of those responsibilities were no longer
hers to bear.
That there was no religious constraint
on her ability
that she could do anything in the world.
That her illiteracy
would be non-existent
and anything she could imagine would be possible.
Again
"What are your life dreams?"
Being asked to answer a question in which
even your utopian society
structured itself in such a way that you remained
the servant
she didn't know how to answer.
I tried again
after some prompting
some vague suggestions
I asked her
"if you could have done anything with your life
Money, family, tradition aside...
What would you have wanted to do?"

144

Her answer
more telling than
reality
she said she would want to help others.
Help children.
Elders.
Build a home for those without.
Provide care for those without.
I wanted to cry.
I had to hold it in.
Because all she has ever known was living for
someone else.

I wanted to ask her
who has ever cared for you
but there's no point to asking a question
that you already know the answer to.
No one has ever cared for her.
Or asked her what she thinks
What she wants.
What she dreams.
It was never an option.

I had one more question.
"If you could go anywhere in the world,

Where would it be?"
Without thought
as if second nature
as if her dreams were more like nightmares
she easily answered
"Kenya"
"Home"
Desire to return after exile
Has haunted her ever since that day in 1972.
Wishing to
have never seen the refugee camps
the air france
rescues to escape
decapitation and slaughter.
She came from a poor low-caste family.
but in Uganda
she lived.
She didn't dare to dream
once they barely evaded Idi Amin
because life still belonged to her.
And that was enough.
"Want go home"
She says.
I can't stop the crying
And

I have to excuse myself and leave.

Interlude

HAVE COURAGE

have COURAGE

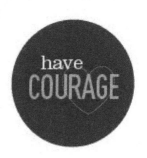

What failures have you experienced? What was that like? What did you learn about yourself or others?

What's something that you've wanted to say but never had the courage to say?

What choices have you made that required courage?

What choices do you know you need to make to be more self-respecting that will require courage?

My Strengths

The most difficult obstacle I ever faced was ...

I overcame it by ...

What I learned about my strengths was ...

Spreading Respect

Write a story about a time when you stood up for yourself or others, without aggression, to spread respect.

Final Thoughts

I'm strong at **Have Courage** because I ...

I can practice **Have Courage** more by ...

My Goals

Practicing "You matter" means having goals regarding our relationships, including family, friends and significant others. Complete the form below to explore your goals *(continued on facing page)*:

	My No. 1 self-care goal is ...	My No. 1 relationship goal is ...	My No. 1 education/career goal is ...
Success looks like:			
Failure looks like:			

Imperfection looks like:			
The most courageous next step is:			
Support I need is:			
I will complete the next step by:			

Chapter 9:

Dialectical Behavioral Therapy

"It's important we communicate"
(Common)

"It's important, we communicate
And tune the fate of this union, to the right pitch"
-Like Water for Chocolate
2000

**Communicating
genuine and authentic
Even as a youth.**

DBT GOALS

- acceptance of needing help
- openness to receive help
- willingness to try

NOT EVEN SUPERHEROES WORK ALONE

In the beginning I used to say
that I was happy I was the one
who had to deal with my combination
of chronic illnesses.
Like I was the only one who could bear it.
Even if it killed me.
Or I killed myself in attempts at survival.
Martyrdom in blasphemy.
As if I was ever that special.

Self imposed distortions of thought in isolation.
Then,
for a little while
I took a break
from going to the doctor to get my lab results.
Most of the time,
after a look at the numbers
and going over all the symptoms
the doctor usually says
with looks of mysticism
'Wow, and you do so much!
You're so strong"

Other teachers at work would say it too.
How amazed they are at my survival.
As if to imply if it were anyone else

they might not be able to handle it.

I'm just not that special.

I have no super powers.
No hidden cape
to move obstacles from paths
no predestined origin to follow.

I'm surviving.

Prehistoric premonitions of intuition.
This incarnate body knows its results.
This body knows suffering.

But I am not surviving alone.

I can't.

Isolation gives power to sickness.

Giving into
navigating blindly through trust because
gas from self combustion is the only thing lighting my
way.
Submitting will to others making
impossible tasks neutralized with vulnerability.

We need help sometimes.
Everyone does.

Sometimes I've asked and found silence.
Each time fearing hurting relationships.
It doesn't change the fact that I still need help.
Not even superheroes work alone.

HELP IS A SPECTRUM

A lady in the ER says to me after I throw up in the
waiting room trash can: "Have you tried making
ginger tea?"
Ba says to me after she hears me throwing up in
the bathroom next to her at 3am: "try ajma "
My roommate in college says to me after I wake her
up throwing up: "I heard fennel can help"
My ex says to me after I call them asking them to
keep me company in the ER: "no"
My mom says to me after being diagnosed with a
chronic illness: "now I understand what it feels like
to do this daily, I'm sorry"
My co-Worker says to me after they see me
struggling to walk: "friend, can I carry your
backpack?"
My roommate says to me after they see my trash
can full of blood: "can I drive you to the ER?"
Someone I used to know says to me after I tell them
I'm suicidal: "don't talk to me about that, it's too
intense"
My Chinese herbalist and acupuncturist says to me
after I ask how many sessions I'll need: "depends,
are you going to learn to manage your stress
better?"

My friend says to me after they help me through a
suicide attempt and breakdown: "I'm not sure things
between us can be like they used to"
The desi man at the check-out stand says to me
after I hand him my ID: "do you know what your
name means?" [hope]
The old guy at the dog park says to me my dog
after he sees my ER tag: "take care of her"
My friend says to me after I share a google doc to a
group with a list of things I need: "I'll just fill in
where everyone else can't"
My partner says to me after I tell them about how
everyone else left because it was just too much:
"I'm not them"
My ancestors say to me after I pray for answers:
"you are the answer"

THE FIRST ROTI IS NOT ALWAYS THE MOST ROUND

Ba has never approved of the roundness of my roti.
I've seen her fix them before she cooks them.
Quickly balling it up and re-doing it,
or folding an edge to make it more perfectly round.
Seen her make remarks under her breath or to my
mother in Gujarati.
Playing the dozens with the dozen i've rolled amongst
their thousands.
Sometimes she just gives me a look and I know.

I know each time I come to the counter to help
it won't be right.
Something will be off and I'll be reminded of it.
I'll even be aware of it as I'm rolling.
Watch the weight distribution push one edge out like a
playground ball kicked too hard,
or the way my mind feels when I try,
step out of my comfort zone,
and fail.
Off.
Oblong.
Looking a little sideways.

Even though I can see she isn't pleased,
she'll never turn me away from trying.

I watch how her wrists push and pull
making the roti spin as it evenly distributes into a
perfect circle
laced with just the right finesse of flour.
It's a dance.
I watch the forearms of experience.
The trauma providing strength
that has been carried with each kneading of dough.
She never had a choice about the roundness of her roti.
She had to perfect the process.

Skills can be developed.
Honed.
I hone in on the skills reminding me to keep trying.
That I have not mastered the skills and need to
continue to practice.
No matter how oval,
or oblong,
or even circular they may turn out.

That no matter what the shape of the roti,
after cooked
the taste is indistinguishable.

Survival is not one size fits all.
Even ba's rotis are not all the same size.
(they are all round though)
I wonder what her first one looked like.

Was is as off as mine?
Hers are so round.*
Encouragement.*
There's hope.*

I'll keep rolling them.*
keep listening to her comments
while crafting my skills.*
keep trying.*
I wont stop trying.*

Chapter 10:

Distress Tolerance

"When the stress burns my brain just like acid rain
drops"
(People Under the Stairs)

"Let the problems in your mind become ancient

artifacts

Perhaps these raps can help you alleviate

The things that's got you trippin' you watch me

demonstrate

First you ignore the nonsense and clear your

conscience

Let your pen touch the paper write verbs and

consonants

As the words become a sentence you start to feelin'

different

The stress is out your mind you feel like the weight

was lifted"

-O.S.T.

2002

Find that thing that helps
But I know it won't always
Coltrane is my one.*

DISTRACTING

ACTIVITIES
Engage in exercise or hobbies

CONTRIBUTING
Contribute to someone/something

COMPARISONS
Check privileges and acknowledge positives you are afforded

EMOTIONS
Read emotional books or stories that evoke the opposite of the emotion you are experiencing

PUSHING AWAY
Push the situation away by leaving it for a while. Leave the situation mentally

THOUGHTS
Count, listen to music, watch TV, read. Get your mind thinking on something else

SENSATIONS
Hold ice in your hand, squeeze a rubber ball, take a hot shower, and listen to loud music

SELF-  SOOTHE

<u>VISION</u>

Look at flowers, change the decoration of a room, light a candle and watch the flame, go to a museum, look at nature, go to a performance. Be mindful of each sight that passes in front of you, not lingering on any specific one.

<u>HEARING</u>

Listen to beautiful music, listen to sounds of nature, play an instrument. Be mindful of any sounds that come your way, letting them go in one ear and out the other.

<u>SMELL</u>

Use your favorite perfumes or lotion, light a scented candle, boil cinnamon, bake cookies or bread, smell the roses. Mindfully breathe in the fresh smells of nature.

TASTE

Have a good meal, a favorite soothing drink (avoid alcohol), treat yourself to a dessert, chew some gum, get a specialty food you don't normally get. Really taste the food you eat mindfully.

TOUCH

Take a bubble bath, put clean sheets on the bed, pet a dog or cat, have a massage, soak your feet, put a cold compress on your forehead, brush your hair, hug someone for longer than 6 seconds. Experience whatever you are touching paying attention to touch that is soothing.

IMPROVE

IMAGERY

Imagine a very relaxing scene. Imagine hurtful emotions draining out of you

MEANING

Find or create some purpose, meaning, or value in the pain. Focus on whatever positive aspects of a painful situation you can find.

RELAXATION

Try muscle relaxing by tensing and relaxing each large muscle group, starting with your hands and arms, going to the top of your head, and then working down; exercise hard; take a hot bath or shower; drink hot milk; massage your neck and scalp, your calves and feet; breathe deeply

ONE THING

Focus your entire attention on just what you are doing right now. Keep yourself in the very moment you are in; put your mind in the present. Focus your entire attention on physical sensations that accompany non-mental tasks (walking, cleaning, fixing, drawing/painting) be aware of how your body moves during each task.

VACATION

Give yourself a brief vacation. Get in bed and pull the covers up over your head for 20 minutes. Rent a room at the beach or in the woods, or go camping. Get a trashy magazine or chocolate and read it in bed. Take a blanket to the park and sit on it for a whole afternoon. Unplug your phone for a day. Take a one-hour break from hard work that needs to be done.

ENCOURAGEMENT

Cheerlead yourself. You are your loudest supporter. I've learned over the years it really is on you and you are the only one who can advocate for yourself.

GUIDELINES FOR ACCEPTING REALITY: BASIC PRINCIPLES OF ACCEPTING REALITY

RADICAL ACCEPTANCE

Pain creates suffering only when you refuse to accept the pain

TURNING THE MIND

Turn from the road of rejecting reality and make an inner commitment to accept. You may have to do this over and over in a span of a few minutes.

WILLINGNESS OVER WILLFULNESS

Do just what is needed in each situation, focus on effectiveness. Listen carefully to your wise mind. Be willing to recognize your connectivity to the universe, earth and ancestors.

Willfulness, on the other hand, is sitting on your hands in time of action, giving up, being ineffective, and trying to fix everything. Choose willingness over willfulness.

OBSERVING-YOUR-BREATH EXERCISES

Focus your attention on your breath, coming in and out. Observe your breathing as a way to center yourself in your wise mind.

Observe your breathing as a way to take a hold of your mind, dropping off non-acceptance and fighting reality.

1. DEEP BREATHING
Lie on your back. Breathe evenly and gently, focusing your attention on the movement of your stomach. As you begin to breathe in, allow your stomach to rise in order to bring air into the lower half of your lungs. As the upper halves

of your lungs begin to fill w air, your chest begins to rise and your stomach begins to lower. Continue for 10 breaths, where the exhalation will be longer than the inhalation.

2. MEASURING YOUR BREATH BY YOUR FOOTSTEPS

Walk slowly in the yard, along a sidewalk, or on a path. Breathe normally. Determine the length of your breath, the exhalation and the inhalation, by the number of steps. Do not force a longer inhalation. Let it be natural. Watch your inhalation carefully to see whether there is a desire to lengthen it. Continue for 10 breaths.

3. COUNTING YOUR BREATH

Sit cross-legged on the floor (sit in the half or full lotus position if you know how); or sit in a chair with your feet on the floor; kneel; lie flat on the floor; or take a walk. As you inhale, be aware that, "I am inhaling, 1". When you exhale, be aware that, "I am exhaling, 1". Remember to breath from the stomach. When beginning the second inhalation be aware that, "I am inhaling 2," slowly exhale aware that, "I am exhaling 2" and so on up to 10. Then return and count back down to 1.

4. FOLLOWING YOUR BREATH WHILE LISTENING TO MUSIC

Listen to a piece of music. Breathe long, light, and even breaths. Follow your breath; be master of it while remaining aware of the movement and sentiments of the music. Do not get lost in the music, but continue to be master of your breath and self.

AWARENESS EXERCISES

1. AWARENESS OF THE POSITIONS OF THE BODY

Begin to focus your attention on your breath. Breathe quietly and more deeply than usual. Be mindful of the position of your body, whether you are walking, standing, lying or sitting down. Know where you walk, stand, lie or sit. Be aware of the purpose of your position. Recognize the ancestral land that you occupy.

2. AWARENESS OF CONNECTION TO THE UNIVERSE

Focus your attention on where your body touches an object (floor, ground, air molecules, chair, bed sheets, clothes, etc.) Try to see all the ways you are connected to and accepted by that object. Consider the function of that object with relation to you. That is, consider what the object does for you. Consider its kindness in doing that. Experience the sensation of touching the object that focuses your entire attention on that kindness until a sense of being connected or loved or cared for arises.

3. AWARENESS WITH MEDITATION

Sit comfortably on the floor with your back straight, laying down or in a chair with both feet toughing the floor. Close your eyes all the way, or open them slightly and gaze at something near. With each breath, say to yourself, quietly and gently one word, over and over. Or instead focus on listening to your heartbeat and nothing else. Try to collect your whole mind and put it into this one objective. When your mind strays, return it gently back to your focus.

Chapter 11:

Emotional Regulation

"Do you wanna talk about it, or be alone?"
(Vince Staples)

"Open up your eyes and tell me whatcha thinkin'
Open up your mind, and tell me whatcha seein'
Inside of me, where I be fussin', fuckin' up this
evenin'
I probably couldn't fix it if I knew the reason
Up on the sea, where I see you fallin' in the deep
end"
-Summertime 06
2015

Stay true to yourself.
Integrity regardless.
Value your values.

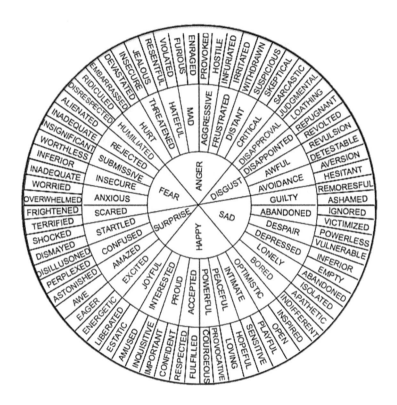

Plutchik's "Wheel of Emotions"

EMOTION AND MINDFULNESS WORKSHEET/CHECK-IN

Select a current or recent emotional reaction and fill out as much of this as you can.

Emotion name:_____
Intensity (0-100):_____

Prompting event for emotion: (who, what where, when) what started the emotion?

Interpretations (beliefs, assumptions, appraisals) of the situation?

Body changes and sensing: What am I feeling in my body?

Body language: What is my facial expression? Posture? Gestures?

Action urges: What do I feel like doing? What do I want to say?

What I said OR did in the situation: (be specific)

What after effect emotion have on me (my state of mind, other emotions, behavior, thoughts, memory, body, etc.)?

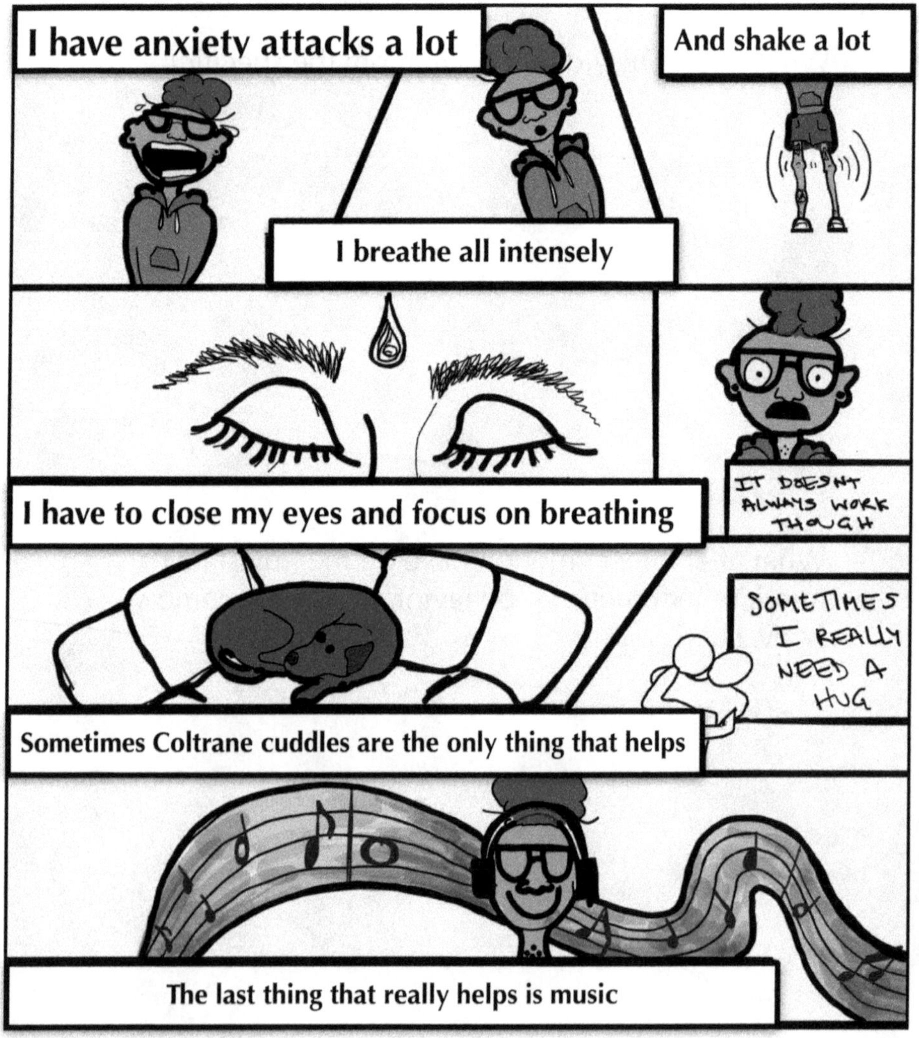
I have anxiety attacks a lot
I breathe all intensely
And shake a lot
I have to close my eyes and focus on breathing
IT DOESN'T ALWAYS WORK THOUGH
Sometimes Coltrane cuddles are the only thing that helps
SOMETIMES I REALLY NEED A HUG
The last thing that really helps is music

EMOTIONAL REGULATION

They called me aggressive again.
I don't know how many times this makes it now.
They said I was intimidating.
That I waved my arms and jumped around.
Trust me,
you would know if I was screaming.
I project because I'm speaking from generations of
silencing.

Tell me to calm down one more time.

The sweat on my upper lip is growing.
I can feel the beads.
I get so hot.
This Aries
Leo rising fire they say.
I don't know,
but I'm hot.

Did they just say that?

Cindy told me that if you drink water,
it dilutes the chemicals in the brain
helping you calm down.
It's not just talk.

Science.

Hydrate.

I swear if I catch them in these streets.

They say they're just trying to help me out.
Trying to let me know slouching in my chair at a staff
meeting
can be perceived as unprofessional.
That the way I licked my lollipop at the catered meeting
was disrespectful.
That my melanin threatened them so much
they had to find something to pick at.

Tell me to relax again.

You can't tell me to breathe
with your knee on my throat.

Striving to
move with purpose.
Grace.
Ancestral guidance.
Controlled burns instead of rage.
Not wild
unwilling to be contained.
Sage.

"Okay, are we done here?
Thank you,
have a nice day"

Chapter 12:

Interpersonal Effectiveness

Can I talk to you? I want to talk to you
(Aaliyah)

"Can I talk to you?
Comfort you
Let you know
I Care 4 U"
-*I Care 4 U*
2002

Sorry Aaliyah
I just wish she had more time.
Jaq called and we cried.

GOALS:
Be skillful in stating your wants and needs

I have vivid memories of when I was little and my parents used to argue, doors would slam and my father would leave

I didn't realize the trauma it had created until I became an adult, and had my own relationships

It was a huge trigger for me, so I had to learn to let people know about it

GOALS:
Build relationships and end destructive ones

After my suicide attempt, I found myself lacking friendships I used to have

I had just met another dope brown educator.

I called her, but no answer. Then I missed a call back from her and I check the voicemail...

It was like she knew I needed someone.

Our friendship instantly turned into one of the most supportive and honest ones I have. I was so scared to reach out, but it made all the difference.

204

GOALS:
Find balance and acceptance in change

PRIORITIES IN INTERPERSONAL RELATIONSHIPS

<u>Objective effectiveness</u>

Stating wants and needs

- Have others take our opinions seriously

<u>Relationship effectiveness</u>

Keeping and improving relationships

- Don't let hurt and problems build up
- Repair relationships when needed
- Resolve conflicts before they get overwhelming
- Find and build new relationships
- End toxic relationships

<u>Self-Respect</u>
<u>effectiveness</u>

Keeping or improving self-respect

- Create and maintain balance in relationships and self

STATING WANTS AND NEEDS:

DESCRIBE
Describe the situation, but stick to the facts. State exactly what you are reacting to.

EXPRESS
Express your feelings and opinions (don't assume the other person knows). Use phrases such as "I want" instead of "you should"

ASSERT
Ask for what you want or say no clearly. Do not assume that others will figure out what you want.

REINFORCE
Explain positive effects of getting what you want or need.

MINDFUL

Keep focus on your goals. Ignore attacks, threats or changes of subject. Just keep making your point. *do not however subject yourself to harmful conversations that show no progress or continue to enforce white supremacy.

APPEARANCE

Appear effective and competent. Use a confident voice, tone, and physical manner. Make eye contact. *this does NOT mean bow down to Eurocentric and heteronormative expectations. Be true to yourself. Have integrity.

NEGOTIATE

Offer and ask for other solutions to the problem. Focus on what will work.

KEEPING THE RELATIONSHIPS:

GENTLE

Be respectful. No attacks, express anger with words. No threats, no "manipulative" statements, no hidden threats. Tolerate "no". No moralizing, abandon blame. Avoid smirking, eye rolling, No cutting off or walking away

INTERESTED

Face the person, maintain eye contact, lean toward the person, and actively listen. Don't interrupt or talk over the person. Be sensitive to the person's wish to have the discussion at a later time. Be patient

VALIDATED

Show that you understand the other person's feeling and thoughts about the situation. Go to a private place when the person is uncomfortable talking in a public place.

Pay attention

Look interested

Reflect back

Say back what you heard the other say, are sure you understand. No judgmental language

Observe

Be sensitive to what is not being said. Pay attention to facial expressions, body language, what is happening, and what you know about the person already.

Understand

Look for how the other person is feeling, thinking or doing makes sense, based on their experiences.

Acknowledge the valid

Look for how the person's feelings, thinking or actions are valid responses because they fit current facts, or are understandable because they are a logical response to current facts

Show humanity

Be yourself. Don't one-up or one-down the other person. Treat them as an equal, not fragile or incompetent

EASY MANNER

Use a little humor. Be light-hearted.

KEEPING RESPECT FOR YOURSELF

HONOR

Be fair to yourself. Remember to validate your own feelings and wishes.

APOLOGIES

Don't over apologize. No apologizing for being alive or making requests. No apologies for having an opinion or disagreeing. No looking ashamed. No invalidating the valid.

INTEGRITY

Stick to your own values. Don't sell out your integrity for reasons that aren't very important. Be clear on what you believe is the moral or valued way of thinking and acting.

AUTHENTICITY

Don't lie. Don't act helpless when you're not. Don't exaggerate or make up excuses.

213

ASSERTIVE BILL OF RIGHTS

I have the right to...

Ask for what I want

Say no to requests or demands that I cannot meet

Express all of my feelings-positive and negative

Change my mind

Make mistakes and do not have to be perfect

Follow my own values and beliefs

Say no to anything if I feel that I am not ready, if it is unsafe, or if it conflicts with my values

Determine my own priorities

Not be responsible for the actions, feelings, or behavior of others

Expect honesty from others

Be angry with someone I love

Be myself and to be unique

Express fear

Say, "I don't know"

Not give excuses or reasons for my behavior

Make decisions based on my feelings on my own personal space and time

VARIATIONS OF
RESPONSES AND STYLES
OF COMMUNICATION

PASSIVE

Always giving into what others
want, doesn't express feelings,
afraid to say no, discounting your own wants and needs

AGRESSIVE

Being demanding, hostile, or rude. Insensitive to the rights of
others, intimidates others into doing what they want,
disrespectful

PASSIVE-AGGRESSIVE

You tell people what they want to hear to avoid conflict,
however you still feel angry inside and don't follow through on
expectations or requests, which can result in resentment. Can
sometimes sound condescending or sarcastic.

MANIPULATIVE

Attempt to get what you want by making others feel guilt, then to play the role of the victim in order to get others to take responsibility for taking care of your needs. We see this a lot in immigrant families. It often looks like shame.

ASSERTIVE

Directly, honestly, and appropriately stating what your thoughts, feelings, needs, or wants are. You take responsibility for yourself and are respectful to others. You are an effective listener and problem solver.

**Being assertive enables people to act in their own best interest. It supports a person to stand up for themselves without mounting anxiety, to express their feelings honestly, and assertively. It facilitates a person to exercise their own personal rights without denying the rights of others.
**Non-verbal behaviors are as important as verbalizing your assertiveness. The signals that a person sends, as well as receives, are crucial to the success of assertive communication. Non-verbal cues include eye contact, body posture, personal space, gestures, facial expressions, and tone of voice, inflection of voice, vocal volume, and timing. Other variables include smile, head nodding, and appropriate animation.

REFLECTION SHEET

Use this reflection sheet to think of a recent or current time in your life where you would like to evaluate your interpersonal effectiveness priorities.

Prompting event for my problem:

Who did what to whom? What led up to what?

What is it about this situation that is a problem for me?

*** *Don't forget to check the facts.* ***

MY WANTS AND DESIRES IN THIS SITUATION

Objectives:

What specific results do I want?

What do I want this person to do, stop or accept?

Relationship:

How do I want the other person to feel and think about me because of how I handle the interaction?

Self-Respect:

How do I want to feel or think about myself because of how I handle the interaction?

My priorities in this situation:

Rate priorities 1(most important)-3(least)

____Objectives

____Relationship

____ Self-respect

Imbalances and conflicts in priorities that make it hard to be effective in this situation:

What I said or did in the situation:

How effective was the interaction?

Interlude

SET BOUNDARIES

set
BOUNDARIES

What boundaries are you willing to set to achieve what matters to you?

What feels in balance versus out of control about your life right now?

What are common situations in which you find yourself feeling resentful towards others? How are your boundaries—or lack of boundaries—connected to these feelings of anger?

How I Can Say No

Three Kinds of Boundaries

- **Assertive** boundaries are the most respectful—to yourself and others. They are clear, direct and focused on your feelings or needs, not the other person.
- **Aggressive** boundaries are argumentative, blaming or might even incite violence.
- **Passive** boundaries are unspoken or dishonest, such as when you expect others to read your mind, you lie or you are vague.

Example: You don't want to go to a party because you have an early commitment the next day and you don't drink alcohol. ASSERTIVE: *I'm not going to the party.* AGGRESSIVE: *I would never go to that party—I don't drink and you shouldn't either!* PASSIVE: *I'll meet you there* (and then you don't show up).

List opportunities or people you know you want to say "no" to in your life right now, and write how you will say it.

Situation	How I will say no

Situation	How I will say no

My Main Boundaries

1. **Get clear on your top boundaries.** What are you saying YES to and what are you saying NO to?

2. **Your values.** What's important to you? What beliefs do you live by?

3. **Self-care.** How can you take care of yourself each day? Remember your goals, how you want to feel and how you want to treat people.

4. Work, school, volunteering and passions. What do you need to stop doing that is stressing you out or making you hate life? What do you love that you want to do more often?

5. Relationships. How do you want to maintain your self-respect when you're around friends, family or boyfriend/girlfriend? Where have you gone past a boundary you need to re-set?

Relationship Boundaries

The relationship that has influenced me most is ...

I think this relationship is healthy (or unhealthy) because ...

Both people communicate with respect (or disrespect) when they ...

Because of this relationship I've learned that ...

Final Thoughts

I'm strong at **Set Boundaries** because I ...

I can practice **Set Boundaries** more by ...

Chapter 13:

Mindfulness

"Nothing less than Hiii Power"
(Kendrick Lamar)

"Everyday we fight the system just to make our way

We've been down for too long, but that's all right

We was built to be strong, 'cause it's our life, na-na-

nah"

-Section.80

2011

**Fuck patriarchy
Must be aware of oneself.*
Save Black Trans Womxn.***

** It should be noted that even though Mindfulness is a new buzzword for many institutions, it is an established ancestral practice, which has been co-opted and commercialized. Tap into your ancestors. Ask them for guidance, focus on them.

What mindfulness is <u>NOT</u>

THE YOGA STUDIO WITH THE OM ON THE WALL

ANYTHING BY DEEPAK CHOPRA

(THERE IS NOTHING MINDFUL ABOUT THIS CHARLATAN)

What mindfulness is <u>NOT</u> pt.2

MINDFULNESS

ANXIETY

A SUPER POWER TO FIX EVERYTHING

PURPOSE:

FINDING AN AWARENESS OF MIND AND
BODY AND LIVING IN THE HERE AND
NOW.

Some of the greatest benefits of mindfulness
come from examining your mental
processes in this way, observing them
dispassionately, as a scientist would.
Because this allows great insight into
habitual ways of thinking, it has a profound
power to alleviate stress and suffering

TAKING A HOLD OF YOUR
MIND

"WHAT" SKILLS

OBSERVE

Notice without getting caught in the experience.
Control your attention, but not what you see

Notice each feeling, rising and falling

Notice what comes through your senses

DESCRIBE

Put words to the experience. When feelings or thoughts arise, acknowledge them

Describe to yourself what is happening. Put a name on your feelings. Call a thought just a thought, a feeling just a feeling. Don't get caught in content.

PARTICIPATE

Enter into your own experience.

Let yourself get involved in the moment, letting go of ruminating

Act intuitively from a wise mind

Actively practice your skills

"WHO" SKILLS

NON-JUDGMENTALLY

See, but don't evaluate.

Take a nonjudgmental stance, just the facts

Unglue your opinions or assumptions from the facts

Accept each moment

Acknowledge the helpful

Acknowledge the hurtful

ONE-MINDFULLY

Do one thing at a time

Let go of distractions

Concentrate on your mind

EFFECTIVELY

Focus on what works

Act as skillfully as you can meeting the needs of the situation
you are in

Keep an eye on your objectives

Let go of vengeance, useless anger, and righteousness that hurts
you and doesn't work

Interlude

BE COMPASSIONATE

be
(COMPASSIONATE)

What is the kindest thing anyone has ever done for you?

When have you needed compassion and not gotten it? What was the impact?

What is the difference between being compassionate and feeling sorry for someone?

What makes you judge people versus get curious about them?

Look Again

When you feel yourself judging and withholding respect—but know deep down that you want to show respect instead—it can help "to look again." Here's how to practice:

1. **Tell Your Truth about your feelings.** When judgment of people strikes your thoughts, name it. Don't judge your feelings or needs, though.

   - I'm feeling [*fill in the blank*] toward [*name*] right now.

   - I feel like I'm not getting what I need, which is …

2. Look again. Pause and consider:

- What shortcomings do you see in   them   that you also see in yourself?
- When have you been painfully misunderstood?
- In what ways are you being hard on   them   in a similar way now?
- What would you need if you were in   their   shoes?

When I look again at this situation, I see ...

3. Pick a Respect Basic. What Respect Basic can you practice in this moment to generate more respect in this situation?

My Role Models

One person I admire for their compassion is ...

I follow his/her example and practice compassion by ...

I can increase my compassion by ...

My Close Relationships

I wish I could understand why people ...

I struggle to feel compassion for the following person ...

I am willing to be more compassionate toward them by ...

Respect Letter

Below, write a letter to someone in your life with whom you want to create a more respectful relationship. Don't blame, shame or complain. Instead, throughout the letter, focus on what you are feeling and needing and include the phrase "I respect you because ..." so that it contains an acknowledgment of their strengths. Suggest how you can create more respect in your relationship and how you want your relationship to be going forward. You can decide whether to share the letter or not—see how just writing the letter helps you generate compassion.

Final Thoughts

I'm strong at **Be Compassionate** because I ...

I can practice **Be Compassionate** more by ...

Chapter 14:

Duality

"It's just me against the world"
(Tupac Shakur)

"The message I stress: to make it stop study your

lessons

Don't settle for less — even the genius asks-es

questions

Be grateful for blessings

Don't ever change, keep your essence

The power is in the people and politics we address

Always do your best, don't let the pressure make you

panic"

-Me Against the World

1995

Don't give up culture
to give into mental health
There has to be space.

Diasporic children are born in dual realities
Called to honor and simultaneously grow.
How can one stay rooted and still evolve?

East and west meet affirmation and validation.
Stress.
The Vagus nerve.
Its science and a feeling all at once.

Sometimes it's data driven.
Chemical combination of intention.
Sometimes it's the weight of entire buildings crushing
the breath
not all are entitled to.
But somehow the aunties think we can still manage it
all.

Privileged with capacity to stop and feel.
To think.
To ask:
didn't our ancestors feel sad?
Did depression have a name before the west?

The generational result of trauma neglected.
Resurrected into indescribable actions and unexplained
arguments.

Craving a clinical dissection of self.
Of lineage diagnosed.
What did our ancestors eat to feed their souls?
What is worth preserving of being sacred
and what fears hold the community back from healing?

We live in dual realties.
Recognizing both medicine and medicinal.
Recognizing both emotional and logical.
Allowing honesty to rest to the top.

Interlude

BE OF SERVICE

be of SERVICE

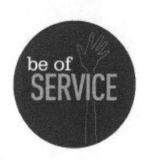

My Purpose

There are things we wish were different in our world. Each of us is a leader in his or her own life. We have to put The Respect Basics into action to change our world. Having courage means we challenge ourselves, know our value and our impact, take risks, make mistakes, learn from them, and try again.

One thing I've survived that is inspiring to others is ...

One form of disrespect I want to help end is ...

The effect of this form of disrespect on myself or others is ...

To **Be of Service** to help end or address this form of disrespect, I will ...

Chapter 15:

Final Reflection

"Keep your eyes on the final hour"
(Lauryn Hill)

"I treat this like my thesis
Well-written topic, broken down into pieces"
-The Miseducation of Lauryn Hill
1998

The album raised me.
Tower Records 10 years old.
It made me feel safe.

Initially, in planning the book, I wanted to write a poem about my journey with creating it, but while I was going through my files I actually found the poem I wrote in 2018, which might have been a suicide note if not for my friends. Thank you Arlene. I found it extremely ironic that as I read it, I could call out the cognitive distortion or the element of my own thinking that was enabling the spiral to form. I am still the person who wrote this, but I have evolved and have gained skills, and tools, and words that I can use to call out the sentiment without invalidating it. It doesn't mean the feelings don't still come up, but remember this is all about management. So, in an effort to showcase growth, here is some of it. I've picked some key lines and excerpts and included them.

CW: suicidal ideation, depression

One time I tried to tell my family about my mental
health

Soulful weight doesn't subside.
Crushing capacity as if these arms
didn't know how to
push back.
These arms
only know how to push back.
They have forgotten how to hold.
Embracing only that which could be detached.
Removed.
Excused.
I'm out of excuses.
Out of masks to tighten on.
The screws all stripped away
of anything left to catch
tools to fasten a facade
that i'm ok.
I'm not.

I had hoped I was wrong.
I sent red flags
left in clear trails to find
something incase
I didn't have breath to show the way.

Depression didn't scare them
slow motioned replays
zoomed in special effects
leaving assumptions left to fill in
sentence frames of confusion.
Mama always told me
"Don't be an imposition"
and I never wanted to take up space.
But there would be moments when
I knew space depended on my survival.
so I would try.
Vacuumed atmospheric
peer pressured into attempts at

authentic existence.
But
you left.
They all left.

So when I finally found the courage to tell my family,
I thought maybe
I could finally be seen

it was easier to just allow them to think
attitude and recluse had no grounds
instead of scratching it passed the surface.
Roots of depression
nestled into soil
so solid.

They could not help me

could not hold me.
My arms no longer had to do any pushing
because my words would do the isolating
all on their own.
These arms don't know how to hold.
But this body
just wants to feel
like it's worth holding.
That days will not go by
before someone realizes
I've disappeared.
As years go on
the isolation
just becomes more and more feasible.

-2018

This is the part of the book where in an ideal world, I'd tell you that if youre reading this, you no longer struggle with any mental health stuff and you know and love yourself fully.

Only, I know that isn't the case. It's taken me about 4 years to make this book. And during that time, I have struggled greatly. I'm struggling as I write this sentence. I do know though, that each time I really started to spiral, I went back to working on the book. It has helped slow me down to analyze exactly what is going on and ask the right questions so that I am more aware.

When I fell out with my best friend of 20+ years in spring 19' for a minute, I went back to the chapters on DBT, so I could better understand my wants and needs and how to express them. It helped me evaluate my feelings and figure out exactly how I wanted to proceed. And when we started talking again after I reached out, I felt like I could navigate the situation without being unsure of myself or the path I wanted to take.

Being assertive is not just good for you, but it helps you do away with some of the ego shit that keeps us from reaching out, or speaking up.

When I lost my job, and subsequent career, as I continue to heal from the trauma of being a queer teacher of color in the public school system in California, aka a target for white supremacists to practice silencing and isolating, I turned to really working on calling out and naming the cognitive distortions that started to manifest in my mind. The absolute and overgeneralized thinking was digging me into a hole that was plotted out for me as soon as I began to speak out against School Resource Officers putting hands on black and brown students. That is to say, sometimes we can speak in absolutes. ACAB. But I needed to be able to delineate between systemic and institutional injustice and how my mind was allocating fault and shame. My mind was playing tricks on me, and with the right tools and validation from my partner, therapist, and closest friends, I could see it for it was: A distortion. I could see reality more clearly. That I was a target of the state because of the way I advocated for BIPOC and queer students. That my story was not in isolation and that I was a part of a larger historical movement to silence agitators who disrupt hegemony and institutionalized hate. It didn't fix anything but at least it contextualized it. By making it less personal, I was able to remove the emotional piece that was keeping me anxious.

Then the pandemic of COVID hit and those feelings of isolation really started to snowball. As an introvert, I admit in the beginning it really didn't hit me too hard, but because access to the people who had always been holding me down was cut off, I started to really need to work on other ways of relieving stress. I also saw this whole thing (still in the pandemic right now) as a way to really work on goal setting, and imagine more radically what is possible.

I chose not to teach back in the classroom this year because I am so scarred. Unemployment of course brings instability and as someone who has had a lot of emergency visits to the hospital, being uninsured was really anxiety inducing for me. I was able to focus on distress tolerance while I figured out how to get signed up for everything. I still go back to distress tolerance when I start to feel anxious about finding my next job, or how long my savings will last.

The global uprising for Black Lives in 2020 has brought a roller coster of emotions. Figuring out your place in the movement has been extremely difficult for a lot of my comrades. We have all discussed the fatigue of doing this work for so long and not seeing much progress, the fatigue of watching people learning something for the first time and all of a sudden being awarded a platform, and the fatigue of committing so much of our capacity to this work that we know is unrelenting.

One thing has become clear as I have been working through the chapter on mindfulness is that I had to stop myself from questioning if I was contributing enough to the current movement. I stopped because I realized that I was using "production," a capitalist tool of measurement, to determine how I was contributing to my community. Thats not the revolution. I had to be mindful, to be more aware of the ways in which I was still traumatized from what happened with the police in schools, and that my impact as a teacher is exponential and not linear. I was able to see my former students at the marches. That kind of "productivity" that isn't measured by capitalism, but by community consciousness. Mindfulness has helped me understand myself better through out this uprising and has helped guide me to where I can contribute the most.

As if the year hadn't already been the worst I've ever experienced, I lost my dog. The only pet I had ever had. The dog I talk about throughout the book as being one of the things that helps me the most. The being that has been the most consistent thing in my life for the last 11 years. He was witness to everything. All of the nights throwing up or bleeding out.

Witness to not being able to get up or walk. Witness to crying without the ability to stop. He knew about all the struggles. He saw me for me though and loved me through all of it. And I lost him. It happened suddenly and I didn't get to say goodbye the way I wanted to. I had to put him down because the cancer was in his lungs and they didn't think he would make it through the night. It still hurts. SO. MUCH. He was truly my everything. This event more than any other has pitted me in a depression I don't know how to fix.

As you could imagine all of this made my chronic health suffer in ways I wasn't prepared, and has put pressure on my relationship that I know isn't sustainable.

There is a deep rooted anger inside of me. Lately it's been hard to figure out what I need. It has turned into frustration and projection and I can tell this isn't something I can keep doing. I need to do the work. To work the book and redefine my value. I need to check in with my ancestors, check my eating habits, and build a playlist. I need to decolonize.

I miss my dog, Coltrane. I can't escape the feelings of loss and I hear you never really do, just that you learn to manage it.

Thats what this whole book is though. It's just a management tool. Sometimes to store your thoughts, and sometimes hopefully to remind you of things you already know, or never gave a name. I already know I'm going to have to keep coming back to this thing. It offers some validation when the path is not so clear. At least, I hope it does. I made it for me, but its for us.

Interlude

GET HELP

get
HELP

What are the biggest challenges you are facing in life today?

What is the impact when you don't ask for the help you need?

What does it feel like to help someone else?

What can you do if someone you ask for help says "no" or is unresponsive?

My Respect Circle

In each circle, write the people, resources, organizations or agencies that could help you. Who can you contact or turn to?

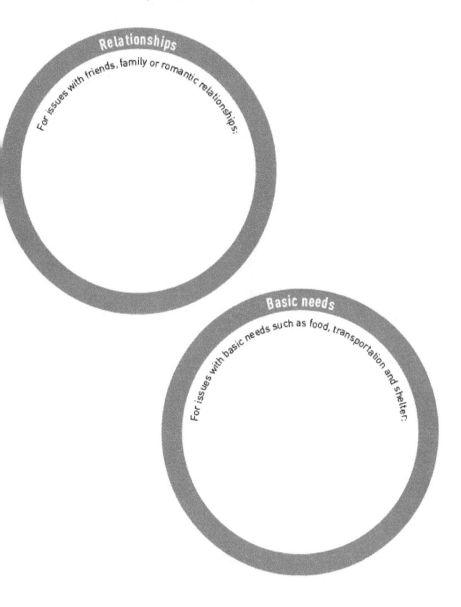

Relationships

For issues with friends, family or romantic relationships:

Basic needs

For issues with basic needs such as food, transportation and shelter:

Education or training

For issues related to learning skills, career goals, or attaining diplomas or certificates:

Emotional and mental health

For issues relating to mental, physical or sexual health:

(such as addictions, depression, self-harm, eating or body image disorders, etc.)

Physical safety

For issues such as violence, bullying or abuse:

78

My Dreams

One big dream I have and why it is important to me is ...

I have gotten help in the past by ...

To make my big dream come true, I need help with ...

One thing I am afraid to ask for help with is ...

One person I trust to help me is ...

One way I can help others to fulfill their dreams is ...

My Recovery

The event that had the biggest negative impact on my life was ...

I got help dealing with it from ...

I can continue to get support when I need it by ...

Final Thoughts

I'm strong at **Get Help** because I ...

I can practice **Get Help** more by ...

Chapter 16:

Notes/Glossary

"With knowledge of self, there's nothing I can't
solve"
(Eric B. & Rakim)

"With knowledge of self, there's nothing I can't solve

At 360 degrees, I revolve"

-Paid In Full

1987

Notes compilation
We only know what we learn.
Write down and reflect.

NEW TERMS

TERM	DEFINITION

NEW TERMS

TERM	DEFINITION

NEW TERMS

TERM	DEFINITION

NOTES/REFLECTIONS

_____

_____

_____

_____

_____

_____

_____

_____

_____

_____

_____

_____

_____

_____

_____

_____

_____

_____

_____

Outro:

Bibliography/Research

"You must learn"
(KRS-One)

"Let me demonstrate the force of knowledge
knowledge reigned supreme
The ignorant is ripped to smithereens"
-Ghetto Music: The Blueprint of Hip-Hop
1989

Always pay homage:
ancestors and intellect.
Experience speaks.

Works Cited and Follow-up Sources

Kaiser Permanente. *Intensive Outpatient Program Manual*, Redwood City Department of Psychiatry, 2018.

BEAM- Black Emotional Mental Health Collective
"Tool Kits & Education." *BEAM*, www.beam.community/tool-kits-education.

National Alliance on Mental Illness
"Home: NAMI: National Alliance on Mental Illness." *NAMI*, www.nami.org/Home.

CBT
Herkov, Michael. "About Cognitive Behavioral Therapy (CBT)." *Psych Central*, 20 June 2019, psychcentral.com/lib/about-cognitive-psychotherapy/.

DBT
Grohol, John M. "An Overview of Dialectical Behavior Therapy." *Psych Central*, 17 May 2020, psychcentral.com/lib/an-overview-of-dialectical-behavior-therapy/.

Teachers of Color
Abolitionist Teaching Network. *Abolitionist Teaching Network*, abolitionistteachingnetwork.org/.

Pet loss
Axelrod, Julie. "Grieving the Loss of a Pet." *Psych Central*, 14 Jan. 2020, psychcentral.com/lib/grieving-the-loss-of-a-pet/.

Open in Emergency 2nd Edition
A hybrid book art project that decolonizes mental health.

The Loveland Foundation
thelovelandfoundation.org

Los Angeles LGBTQ Center
LA LGBT Center Mental Health Services

IG Accounts
@CutiePOCmentalhealth
@TherapyforLatinX
@LatinXtherapist
@Counseling4allseasons
@The.love.therapist
@browngirlselfcare
@teacherselfcareconference

ABOUT THE AUTHOR

IN GUJARATI MEANING HOPE AND SWAHILI

MEANING LIFE

ASHA is an Artist, Educator, and Revolutionary.

Originally from LA, ASHA has been a public school teacher for the last 10 years in the bay area. She is an international poet, striving to use art to create radical change.

ASHA was featured on the cover of Content Magazine, and KQED Arts produced a documentary on her intention and process as an artist. She has showcased her work at many of the prominent poetry events in the Bay Area, as well as been an active speaker, emcee, and performer at numerous rallies and marches for civil and human rights. Her Tedx tells her own personal story of identity through poetry. She is also the author of Crawling in my Skin.

She was given the Hank Hutchins award by the Santa Clara County Alliance of Black Educators for supporting black youth. Her dream is to establish her own K-12 school rooted in restorative practices, art and social justice based standards.

Asha consistently uses her platform to voice out against injustice and to speak up for those who have been marginalized and silenced for centuries.

Contact the author:

IG: @asha_poet

contactASHApoet@gmail.com

www.ASHApoet.com

CPSIA information can be obtained
at www.ICGtesting.com
Printed in the USA
FSHW020406180521
81564FS

9 780578 798868